BIBLE EXPLORERS

EYES · EARS · NOSES HERE COMES MOSES

EXPLORING THE BODY THROUGH THE STORY OF MOSES

Written by Karen Rosario Ingerslev
Illustrated by Kristina Abbott

PURE&FIRE

As Moses' FEET
stood on holy ground

Darkness, tiredness, itchy TOE

"Come on Pharaoh, let us go!"

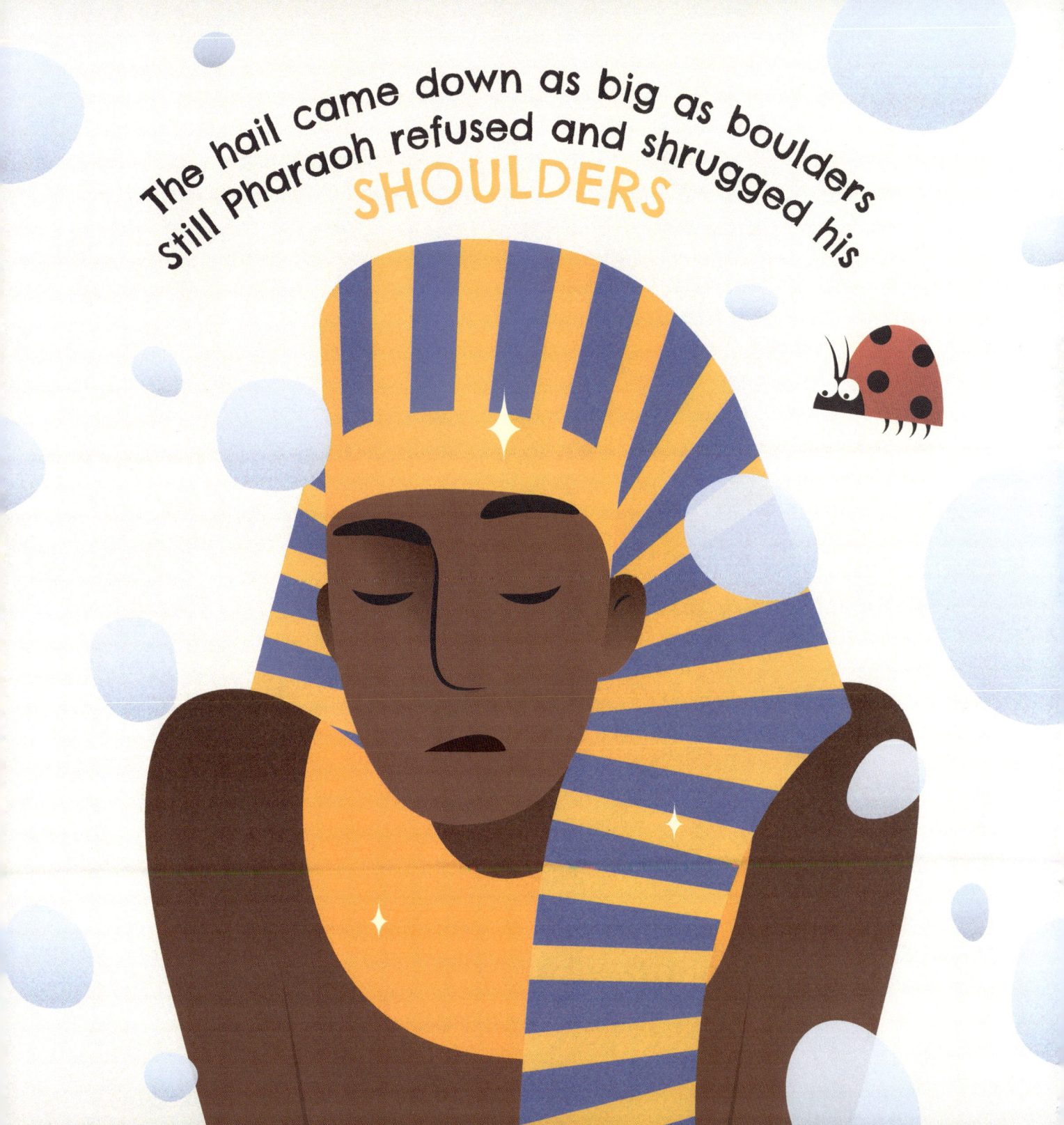

Blood in the river and cows falling ill Pharaoh rubbed his **CHIN** until...

The worst plague of all was sent from God's HAND

And weeping and wailing filled the land

But when they reached the sea
they stopped in their tracks
Pharaoh's army was following
behind their BACKS

Their LEGS trembled,
they could hardly stand
But God always has a plan

God parted the sea and they walked through unharmed

For Emma

K.R.I

Text copyright © Karen Rosario Ingerslev 2022
Illustrations copyright © Kristina Abbott 2022
www.kristinadesign.co.uk

The right of Karen Rosario Ingerslev to be identified as the author and of Kristina Abbott to be identified as the illustrator of this work has been asserted by them in accordance with the Copyright, Designs and Patents Act 1988.

All rights reserved.
No part of this publication may be reproduced or transmitted in any form or by any means — electronic, mechanical, photocopying, recording, or any information storage or retrieval system — without prior written permission from the publisher.

Eyes · Ears · Noses, Here Comes Moses

BIBLE EXPLORERS

First published in the UK by Pure & Fire in 2022
Pure & Fire, England
www.pureandfire.com

ISBN: 978-1-915699-02-2
Also available as an eBook

Printed in Great Britain
by Amazon